FACET BOOKS

HISTORICAL SERIES

FACET fb BOOKS

HISTORICAL SERIES—4

Clarence L. Lee, Editor

Jerusalem and Rome

The Problem of Authority
in the Early Church

by

HANS VON CAMPENHAUSEN

and

HENRY CHADWICK

Lincoln Christian College

FORTRESS PRESS   PHILADELPHIA

The Authority of Jesus' Relatives in the Early Church
was first published as
Die Nachfolge des Jakobus in *Aus der Frühzeit des Christentums*
(Tübingen: J. C. B. Mohr [Paul Siebeck], 1963),
and is published here by arrangement with the publisher.
The English translation is by G. W. Luetkeholter.

The Circle and the Ellipse:
Rival Concepts of Authority in the Early Church
was first published by Oxford University Press, England, in 1959
and is reprinted here by arrangement with the publisher.

3790G66   Printed in U.S.A.   UB3031

Introduction

THROUGHOUT the history of the church, the problem of authority has often assumed interesting geographical and hereditary dimensions. A notable example of the former can be seen in the consolidation of authority in the churches of Rome and Constantinople, a development which is inseparable from the fact that these churches were located in the chief cities of the later Roman Empire. Many other examples could be cited of how ecclesiastical authority—doctrinal, liturgical, and jurisdictional—has tended to become associated with certain cities and territories. Although the church has never been able to agree concerning the nature and extent of the authority inherent in geographical location, and frequently has refused to admit the existence of this dimension of authority, the factor of geography must be credited with having played a decisive role in determining the locus of ecclesiastical authority from the very beginnings of the church's life.

The hereditary dimension of ecclesiastical authority, on the other hand, can be seen most clearly perhaps in the theory of apostolic succession. According to this theory, certain individuals in the church are believed to have inherited the distinctive privileges and charismata given to the apostles of the Lord. Heredity involves here, of course, a purely spiritual type of descent or "pedigree," but the question of authority is made to depend nevertheless upon the perpetuation of a certain

61334

lineage or "family" in the life of the church. Although the inherited authority of the apostle has been by far the most significant in the history of the church, numerous other attempts have been made to establish positions of authority in the church by tracing the spiritual ancestry of certain functionaries or officials back to specially revered and authoritative individuals.

The following essays by Hans von Campenhausen and Henry Chadwick concern the effect which geographical and hereditary factors had in determining the locus of authority in the earliest stages of the church's development. In a sense, the problem of where and in whom the leadership of the church should be located was the most crucial problem which the early church faced. The very existence of the church as an institution depended upon the discovery of viable forms of leadership which could regulate and direct the church in the crisis-filled years of its early life. Moreover, the resolution of the problem of authority by the early church has proved to be just as crucial for the subsequent history of the church, for in defining and locating the lines of authority and leadership for its own day, the early church, in effect, determined the pattern of authority which the church has followed throughout a large part of its history. It is of the greatest importance, therefore, that we examine the issues and factors which were involved in the early church's approach to the problem of authority.

Von Campenhausen's study deals primarily with the hereditary dimension of early Christian leadership, specifically with the intriguing possibility that one of the earliest attempts to locate an authoritative leadership for the church may have involved a succession of the actual blood relatives of Jesus. Such a theory concerning the leadership of the Palestinian Christian community was made popular in the early years of the present century by the great German scholar, Adolf von Harnack. Von Harnack claimed to find in the early accounts of the kinsmen of Jesus something closely resembling the later

Mohammedan caliphate, that is, a dynastic type of leadership based upon a blood relationship to the "prophet" or founder of the religious community. The theory continues on in our day in the work of many outstanding scholars and undoubtedly will always have its advocates.

Von Campenhausen, himself, is disinclined to find a succession of leadership inherent in the descendants of Jesus. While everyone may not find his arguments against the theory completely convincing, he does provide one of the most thorough and lucid examinations of the problem from all sides. Most important, his study clearly establishes that heredity, in a biological sense, was never a major concern of the early church in its search for authority. Even if there had been a brief period when authority was identified with the relatives of Jesus—a phenomenon which von Campenhausen finds hard to believe—it would have been an altogether "exotic" development, hardly representative of what the early church as a whole was doing to solve the problem of authority.

The companion essay by Henry Chadwick reveals the kind of hereditary succession which did prove to be a significant factor in locating authority in the early church. Where hereditary concerns existed, it was not blood relationship but spiritual ancestry which was made the criterion for ecclesiastical leadership. Chadwick documents this principle in terms of the most impressive ancestry in the early church, that of Rome, which included the names of the two most illustrious apostles, Peter and Paul. No other church which accepted the principle that ecclesiastical leadership depended upon an orderly succession of apostolic authority could hope to rival the commanding position which Rome enjoyed by virtue of its apostolic foundations.

Actually, however, Chadwick's study is more concerned to demonstrate the geographical dimension of the problem of authority in the early church. The emergence of the Roman church as the leading church of the early Christian world, Chadwick shows, was closely related to the mystique of leadership which was associated with the city of Rome and which tended to pass over to any institution which was located there. In order to assert its leadership, however, Rome was forced to challenge the authority of another city which also possessed a powerful mystique for the early Christian world.

This city, of course, was Jerusalem. Originally, as an exclusively Jewish movement, primitive Christianity found its geographical center quite naturally in Jerusalem, a city which was also the center of the Jewish world. As the church gravitated more and more toward the Gentile world, however, Jerusalem's position as the center of leadership for the church became less and less tenable. Rival centers of leadership arose which were more strategically located in terms of the changed conception of the Christian mission. The memory of Jerusalem's original pre-eminence lived on in the church, but the actual leadership of the church withdrew almost completely from the city of its origins and came to reside in other cities of the ancient world.

Of all the cities in the Gentile world, no city could provide the kind of authority which was inherent in the Roman church's geographical location. Even as the Jewish world looked to Jerusalem for leadership, the Gentile world was accustomed to look to Rome. This fact, plus the impressive apostolic pedigree which the Roman church possessed, gave that church an advantage which it was quick to exploit. Out of this combination of ideal circumstances came the reality of papal authority, an authority which in many respects was and is the product of geography and heredity.

Hans von Campenhausen was born in 1903. He was educated at the universities of Marburg, Heidelberg, and Berlin, and since 1945 has been professor of ecclesiastical history at Heidelberg. He is recognized as one of the leading authorities on the early church. Unfortunately, few of his major writings, including the extremely important work *Kirchliches Amt und geistliche Vollmacht*, have been translated into English. He is perhaps best known in this country through the two volumes

Fathers of the Greek Church and *Fathers of the Western Church* which contain brief surveys of the lives and works of the more important Fathers of the early church.

Henry Chadwick was born in 1920. He was educated at Eton and Cambridge, and since 1959 has been Regius Professor of Divinity and Canon of Christ Church, Oxford. Some of his more important publications are *Origen, Contra Celsum, The Sentences of Sextus and St. Ambrose on the Sacraments.* He is the co-author of the volume *Alexandrian Christianity* in the Library of Christian Classics, and has been a frequent contributor to learned journals and periodicals.

CLARENCE L. LEE

Lutheran Theological Seminary
Philadelphia, Pennsylvania
Fall, 1966

Contents

THE AUTHORITY OF JESUS' RELATIVES IN THE EARLY CHURCH

by Hans von Campenhausen

IN Christianity physical descent and spiritual kinship seem
to have little to do with each other. This is why accounts that
the brothers and other relatives of Jesus enjoyed a unique
prominence in the Palestinian Christian community are especially interesting. These accounts seem to be the nuclei of an
entirely different line of development than that upon which
the church later embarked. Ever since Harnack tried to apply
the "idea of a caliphate"[1] exercised by James, the brother of
the Lord, to the structure of the primitive church, this idea
has been repeatedly under discussion. J. Weiss,[2] R. Knopf,[3]
Burnett Hillman Streeter[4] and others more or less take this
idea into consideration in their presentations of primitive Christianity. E. Meyer calls attention to similar parallels not only

[1] Adolf von Harnack, *Entstehung und Entwicklung der Kirchenver-
fassung und des Kirchenrechts in den ersten zwei Jahrhunderten* (Leipzig, 1910), p. 26.

[2] Johannes Weiss, *Das Urchristentum* (Göttingen, 1917), pp. 558 ff.

[3] Rudolf Knopf, *Das apostolische Zeitalter* (1905), pp. 25 ff.

[4] Burnett Hillman Streeter, *The Primitive Church* (New York: Macmillan Co., 1929), pp. 39 ff.

in Mohammedanism, but also in Mormonism.[5] In one of his books even Goguel, who is highly skeptical about these reports concerning the Lord's relatives, devotes a section to the idea of a caliphate entitled "James and Dynastic Christianity." [6] To my knowledge the only exception is Lietzmann. He seems to treat the idea to a much lesser extent and with a guarded statement.[7] He does not document his statement and it is uncertain to what extent he wishes to differ from his forerunners.[8] The most recent portrayal of Jewish Christianity by H. J. Schoeps revives the idea of a primitive Christian caliphate[9] and believes that the Jewish-Christian Pseudo-Clementine epistles contain a great many Messianic-dynastic concepts.[10]

I do not believe that we are justified in assuming that any such idea of a caliphate existed anywhere in primitive or in later Jewish Christianity. The Jewish concept of the family and of the inheritable character of spiritual dignity[11] make this idea a remote possibility. But a remote possibility may not be construed as a fact. The idea that the dynasty of Jesus exercised a caliphate is based upon a combination of three accounts or groups of accounts which demand our scrutiny. They deal with: (1) the esteem which Jesus' relatives enjoyed in the early church down through the second (or even third) century as *desposunoi* [those belonging to the Master]; (2) the "monarchical," prominent position to which James, the

[5] Eduard Meyer, *Ursprüng und Anfänge des Christentums*, III (Stuttgart, 1923), 224 f.

[6] Maurice Goguel, *La naissance du christianisme* (Paris, 1946), pp. 129 ff., cf. also pp. 170 ff.; and *L'Eglise primitive* (Paris, 1947), pp. 33, 99 f.

[7] Hans Lietzmann, *Geschichte der alten Kirche* (4th ed., 1961), p. 58.

[8] Lietzmann refers especially to the works of Harnack and Edward Meyer. However, he also regards Symeon as the "successor" of James.

[9] Hans Joachim Schoeps, *Theologie und Geschichte des Judenchristentums* (Tübingen, 1949), pp. 282 f.

[10] *Ibid.*, p. 126.

[11] See also: Adolph Schlatter, *Die Kirche Jerusalems vom Jahre 70-130* (2nd ed., Gütersloh, 1898), pp. 22 ff.; especially Joachim Jeremias, *Jerusalem zur Zeit Jesu*, II B (Göttingen, 1958), pp. 17 ff., pp. 77 ff.; and N. A. Dahl, *Das Volk Gottes* (1941), p. 575.

brother of the Lord achieved in the later primitive congregation; and (3) the successors of James—i.e., relatives who are said to have succeeded to his position precisely because they were his blood relatives. The acceptance of the idea of a caliphate hinges on this last point, and it is to this point that we must devote our chief attention. As for the first two points, it suffices to say that in themselves they prove nothing about a caliphate.

I

Apparently Jesus' brothers[12] were not disciples during his earthly life.[13] It seems that they became identified with the Christian congregation only after his resurrection.[14] Along with the disciples these relatives enjoyed an exceptional prominence in this congregation. Paul knew that these relatives, as well as Peter, took their wives along with them on journeys. He also knew that the congregations which they visited provided hospitality for them.[15] Judging from the context, we must assume that the journeys were evangelism tours, or a combination of evangelizing-inspection visitations in Galilee or in other predominantly Jewish-Christian areas.[16] According to a later account of Julius Africanus, relatives of the Lord "from the Jewish villages of Nazareth and Kokhaba traveled throughout the land," attempting to authenticate their lineage by a genealogical book entitled *The Book of Days*. In line with the belief prevalent in the church concerning Jesus' lineage, these relatives considered themselves descendants of

---

[12] Theodor Zahn, *Forschung zur Geschichte des neutestamentlichen Kanons und der altkirchlichen Literatur*, VI, P. II: "Brüder und Vettern Jesu" (Leipzig, 1900), pp. 225 ff. is a basic and indispensable work on this subject. L. Hermann's "La famille du Christ d'après Hegésippe," in *Revue de l'université de Bruxelles*, 42 (1936/37), 387-94, contains no new material.

[13] Mark 3:21, 31 and parallels; Mark 6:3 and parallels; cf. also John 7:6, 10.

[14] Acts 1:14.

[15] I Cor. 9:5.

[16] Cf. Ernst Lohmeyer, *Galiläa und Jerusalem* (1936), pp. 53 f.; p. 57 contains many far-fetched combinations and unsubstantiated inferences.

David. For this reason two of these relatives were tried in Rome during the reign of Domitian as alleged royal pretenders. In Rome it was soon proved that these two relatives were just poor farmers, not revolutionary conspirators. They were men whose hope was fixed on a "heavenly, angelic kingdom." They were released unharmed.[17] Nonetheless, during the reign of Trajan a certain Symeon, another relative of the Lord, is said to have been suspected of plotting an insurrection and to have been crucified. Hostile Jewish "sects" [18] were said to have made the charges against Symeon.[19] The details concerning this case are highly legendary,[20] and the intervention by Roman officials does not warrant the conclusion that the accused relatives really claimed or actually held a monarchical position in their church. In the case of the two relatives tried under Domitian, such a claim to monarchical position is ruled out precisely because two men were involved. When Hegesippus, to whom we are indebted for these accounts, adds his own comment that these men thereafter "occupied a prominent rank throughout the entire church as martyrs and blood relatives of the Lord," [21] or were held in high esteem, we may not interpret this manner of speaking in the organizational-hierarchical sense of an office or of a dynastic rank.[22] From all

[17] Hegesippus in Eusebius, *Historia Ecclesiae*, III, 20, 1-6.

[18] Adolph Schlatter, *op. cit.*, p. 27, makes it probable that Hegesippus understood *aireseis* to mean the Jews. Cf. Eusebius, *Historia Ecclesiae*, IV, 22, 5 and Schlatter, p. 145.

[19] Hegesippus in Eusebius, *op. cit.*, III, 32, ⟨

[20] E.g., torture prolonged over a period of many days; the amazement of the proconsul, and the martyr's extremely advanced age (120 years). If the period of torture is accepted as a fact, then this would indicate a trial for being a Christian rather than a trial for high treason.

[21] Eusebius, *op. cit.*, III, 32, 6. Cf. also III, 20, 8.

[22] Cf. Zahn, *op. cit.*, p. 300. Harnack is of the opinion that it is impossible "to understand *proegountai* simply as an expression of general high esteem." Rather it is an "esteem equal to that of the apostles." Cf. Adolf von Harnack, *Die Mission und Ausbreitung des Christentums in den ersten drei Jahrhunderten* (4th ed., 1924), p. 633, n. 2. But it is impossible to believe that the term "rule" would have so technical a meaning by the second century. The *proegoumenoi* are simply those who are honored and the *protokathedritai* of the congregation, as in

of this just this much is clear: in the early Jewish-Christian church blood relationship to Jesus counted as a high honor, and combined with other qualities, conferred prestige and prominence. Legendary accounts label another martyr[23] and three Seleucid bishops of the third century[24] as relatives of the Lord. But there is no tradition to the effect that the *desposunoi* as such ever laid claim to the government of the church or that they ever had a member of family as a superior who ostensibly could have exercised monarchical authority.

II

James, the brother of the Lord, is the only relative of Jesus who doubtlessly occupied a towering (quasi monarchical, if you will) position in the primitive church. But even James did not become one of the congregation until after the resurrection. Nonetheless he soon attained to a prominent position along with Peter and John—ultimately the leading position.[25] The Book of Acts eventually depicts James as the head of the Jerusalem congregation and of its presbytery.[26] The reason for this is that James represented the Jewish wing of the primitive congregation[27] which became the dominant element

Shepherd of Hermas, Vision III. In the third century it is the martyrs who occupy places of honor in the congregations next to the presbyters as the official leaders. It is very plausible that the two confessors who were members of Jesus' family were elders in the Palestinian congregation, but it is not an absolute certainty.

[23] *Martyrium Conon,* 4, 2; in addition, Harnack, *Geschichte der altchristlichen Literatur bis Eusebius, II: Chronologie II* (2nd ed.; Leipzig, 1958), pp. 469 f.

[24] *Gregor Barhebraeus, Chronica ecclesiastica,* III f. (in Zahn, *op. cit.,* p. 295, n. 1).

[25] In Gal. 1:18 Paul still regards Peter as the most important person in the Jerusalem congregation. In Gal. 2:9 (according to the correct reading) James takes precedence over Peter and John in the list of *stuloi;* and in 2:12 Peter "drew back and separated himself" before "certain men" sent by James. Cf. H. Strathmann, "Die Stellung des Petrus in der Urkirche" in *Zeitschrift für Systematische Theologie,* 20 (1943), 243 f.

[26] Acts 15:13; 21:18.

[27] Gal. 1:19.

in the primitive congregation after the dispersion of the Hellenists[28] and the departure of Peter.[29] If we ask on what grounds James's considerable authority up to this point was based, the answer is that in addition to his own outstanding personal characteristics (which are unknowable to us), he was the Lord's brother according to the flesh. All that Josephus could say in his comment about the murder of James was that "the brother of Jesus, the so-called Christ, was named James." [30] But the decisive factor which accounts for the esteem in which James was held in the primitive church was not this matter of blood kinship, but something entirely different.[31] After the resurrection Jesus himself appeared to James.[32] This appearance must have been not only James's conversion, but also his "call." [33] For the primitive congregation this put James on a par with the great, primary witnesses of the resurrection, and in this context his name was delivered to Paul, and through him to all Pauline congregations as "of first importance." [34] It is this appearance of Jesus to James which is behind the tendency of later Jewish-Christianity to

[28] Acts 8:11; 11:19.

[29] Acts 12:17. His reappearance and that of the Twelve in Acts 15:6 f. can hardly be historically accurate.

[30] Josephus Flavius, *Jewish Antiquities*, XX, 9, 200. Concerning the authenticity of this debated text see Goguel, *op. cit.*, pp. 145 ff.

[31] Karl Holl has demonstrated this in "Der Kirchenbegriff des Paulus in seinem Verhältnis zu dem der Urgemeinde" in *Gesammelte Aufsätze*, II (Tübingen, 1928), 44 ff. Also, Gerhard Kittel, "Der geschichtliche Ort des Jakobusbriefes" in *Zeitschrift für die neutestamentliche Wissenschaft*, 41 (1942), 74.

[32] I Cor. 15:7.

[33] Holl tries to buttress this thesis by assuming that after the first appearance, which was granted to James alone, a second followed which included James among the apostles. He interprets the *apostoloi pantes* of I Cor. 15:7 to mean the Twelve plus James. This interpretation is untenable. Cf. W. G. Kümmel, "Kirchenbegriff und Geschichtsbewusstsein in der Urgemeinde und bei Jesus" in *Symbolae Biblicae Upsalienses*, 1 (1943), 3 ff.; and Hans von Campenhausen, "Der urchristliche Apostelbegriff" in *Studia Theologica*, I (1947), 105 ff.

[34] I Cor. 15:3.

elevate James not only above Paul, but also above Peter and the other apostles.[35] James's encounter with the risen Christ is put at the beginning and regarded as the primary and fundamental encounter, so that he appears to be the only one of the apostles who never doubted, but who confidently expected the resurrection.[36] Furthermore, the titles given to James do not emphasize his kinship to the Lord but point in another direction. Because of his ascetic life and devotion to the law James is more generally called *ho dikaios* ("the righteous one").[37] He also has the rather puzzling title of *Oblias*, which is supposed to mean "the people's shield." [38] In the not too reliable legend of the martyrdom of James transmitted by Hegesippus, James is portrayed not only as a "holy" Nazarite[39] but also as a truly priestly figure. Only he was permitted to enter the holy of holies garbed in the prescribed linen vestment, there to offer "perpetual intercession" [40] for the sins of his people. Here "the righteous one" appears as a final holy ambassador of God to his stiff-necked people, and is comparable to the great and pious men and intercessors of the Old Testament, whose memory in this respect was very vivid in

[35] This tendency is especially apparent in the admittedly disputed Jewish-Christian sources of the Pseudo-Clementine literature. Cf. Carl Schmidt, *Studien zu den Pseudo-Clementinen* (Leipzig, 1929), especially pp. 322 ff.

[36] Jerome, *De viribus illustribus*, 2.

[37] This designation is standard not only in Hegesippus, but also in *The Hypotyposen* of Clement of Alexandria. Eusebius, *op. cit.*, II, 1, 3-5.

[38] Hegesippus in Eusebius, *op. cit.*, II, 23, 7; cf. also, III, 7, 8. Hans Joachim Schoeps "Jakobus ho dikaios kai oblias" in "Aus frühchristlicher Zeit" in *Religionsgeschichtliche Untersuchungen* (1950), pp. 120 ff. On page 301 Schoeps says that the word is "possibly Hegesippus' confused equation of *seliah* with *apostolus*."

[39] Eusebius, *op. cit.*, II, 23, 5. Cf. Epiphanius, *Haereses,* XXIX, 4; LXXVIII, 7.

[40] Eusebius, *op. cit.*, II, 23, 6. Epiphanius (*Haereses*, LXXVIII, 14) has elaborated still further upon this and made James a high priest. In view of Harnack's footnote in *Chronologie*, I (1897), 186, it does not seem likely that Epiphanius derived this exaggerated nonsense from Hegesippus.

later Judaism.[41] James's murder is supposed to have been fore-told in the Old Testament[42] and the fall of Jerusalem was alleged to be the direct punishment for his murder. With this allusion the account closes on an edifying note.[43]

III

On the basis of the sources dealt with thus far, there is nothing to warrant the idea that James had a successor. This idea of a "successor" begins to appear only when James be-comes a "bishop." [44] In other words, the idea [of a successor to James] is bound up with the dogmatic-polemical concept of a universal succession of bishops as this idea of [episcopal] succession was developed against the Gnostic in the second century. Hegesippus, who is the source of most of the reports about James and the relatives of the Lord, plays a prominent role in this development, and the tendentious nature of his accounts regarding the alleged succession of James is most apparent. This must be demonstrated briefly.

A very clear picture of Hegesippus' significance and effec-tiveness in ecclesiastical politics is given in Caspar's studies and discussions of the list of Roman bishops.[45] According to Cas-par's studies, Hegesippus, "who devoted his life to the struggle against heretics," [46] is regarded as the spiritual father of the

[41] N. Johansson, *Parakletoi: Vorstellungen von Fürsprechern für die Menschen vor Gott in der alttestamentlichen Religion im Spätjudentum und im Urchristentum* (Lund, 1940), pp. 75 ff.; also Ethelbert Stauffer, "Zur Vor- und Frühgeschichte des Primatus Petri," in *Zeitschrift für Kirchengeschichte*, 62 (1943/44), 3 ff.

[42] On this point see Hans Joachim Schoeps, *Theologie und Geschichte des Judenchristentums* (1949), pp. 246 and 359 f.

[43] Eusebius, *op. cit.*, II, 23, 18.

[44] This is not only the case in the pertinent passages of Hegesippus, but also of Clement of Alexandria. Eusebius, *op. cit.*, II, 1, 3 (*Hypotyposen*).

[45] Erich Caspar, *Die älteste römische Bischofsliste* (1926); also, "Die älteste römische Bischofsliste" in *Papsttum und Kaisertum* (1926), pp. 1 ff.; and *Geschichte des Papsttums*, I (1930), 8 ff.

[46] Walter Bauer, *Rechtgläubigkeit und Ketzerei im ältesten Christen-tum* (Tübingen, 1934), p. 111.

lists of bishops.[47] It is possible that he was a Jewish Christian[48] from the East (though hardly from Palestine),[49] who journeyed from congregation to congregation in the latter half of the second century. Wherever he went he entrenched the tradition derived from the apostles and secured that tradition against heretical innovations by grounding his claims in the unbroken continuity of the tradition manifested in the line of monarchical bishops. To him heretical deviations appear to be later detours from the correct path. In the golden era of the apostolic age there were no heresies. In line with this kind of thinking Hegesippus employed the same pattern as that employed by Irenaeus, his somewhat younger contemporary, for the "conviction and refutation" of all heresy, and which from that time on became predominant in the Catholic church.[50] But unlike Irenaeus, Hegesippus emphasized the importance of the successions, although he did not produce any extensive lists. If he had produced such lists, Eusebius certainly would not have neglected to mention them.[51] Apparently Hegesippus was not content with just asserting the continuity of Catholic tradition against the heretics; he occasionally cited names and transitions. An example of this has been preserved in his reference to Rome. There Hegesippus substantiates the continuation of the tradition not only because the tradition in Rome agrees with that of other congregations and with the primitive

[47] Karl Heussi, *War Petrus in Rom?* (1936), pp. 45 ff.

[48] In *Historia Ecclesiae*, IV, 22, 8, Eusebius draws this conclusion on the basis of Hegesippus' knowledge of some Hebrew, but gives no details.

[49] His gross ignorance of the situation there speaks against this possibility. Cf. von Harnack, *Chronologie*, I, p. 312, and Schlatter, *op. cit.*, p. 30, n. 1.

[50] Cf. Bauer, *op. cit.*, pp. 3 f.

[51] This line of argument goes back to Harnack's deductions, once drawn against Lightfoot, in *Chronologie*, I, 180 ff. In the light of new discoveries brought about by scholarly research, Harnack's thesis is preferable to that of C. H. Turner's "The early episcopal lists IV," *Journal of Theological Studies*, 18 (1917), 119 ff., and E. Kohlmeyer's, "Zur Ideologie des "ältesten Papsttums: Sukzession und Tradition," *Theologische Studien und Kritiken*, 103 (1921), 241 f.

Christian norms "dating back to Anicetus," but also, he immediately adds, because Eleutheros had been the deacon of Anicetus, and that Soter succeeded Anicetus and Eleutheros succeeded Soter.[52] Hegesippus does not make such far-reaching assertions about Corinth. He mentions only Primus, the last bishop whom he knew personally.[53] But it is quite conceivable that Hegesippus went back even further in other instances where he believed himself to be accurately informed. Above all it is clear that he sought to establish a point of historical contact with the apostles themselves, from whom all correct catholic doctrine supposedly issued.[54] It is in this context that we must understand the fragment which speaks of Symeon as the bishop who succeeded James. Hegesippus writes:[55]

> After James laid down his life as a witness under the same charge as that made against the Lord,[56] Symeon, the son of James's uncle Clopas, was installed as bishop. He was unanimously nominated because he was the Lord's cousin and was the second bishop.[57] This is why up to this time the Church was called a virgin, for the Church was as yet undefiled by vain doctrine.[58] But then Thebathis began to defile the Church because he had not become bishop. He came from the seven sects of the (Jew-

[52] Eusebius, *op. cit.*, IV, 22, 3. On the concept of *diadoche*, cf. in addition to Caspar, *op. cit.*, T. Klauser, "Die Anfänge der römischen Bischofsliste," in *Bonner Zeitschrift für Theologie und Seelsorge*, 8 (1931), 193-213.

[53] Eusebius, *op. cit.*, IV, 22, 2.

[54] E. Buonaiutis' fantastic assumption that Hegesippus gave its present form to Peter's statement in Matt. 16:18 needs no refutation. Cf. his article, "Marcione e Egesippo" in *Religio*, 12 (1936), 401-13.

[55] Eusebius, *op. cit.*, IV, 22, 4-6.

[56] For an explanation of this introductory sentence see Hans von Campenhausen, *Die Idee des Martyriums in der alten Kirche* (1936), p. 85, n. 3.

[57] The *deuteron* of the text cannot be made to refer to *anepsion*, but to *episkopon* (as is the case in Eusebius in *Historia Ecclesiae*, III, 22). Cf. Zahn, *op. cit.*, p. 237; and Hermann, *op. cit.*, p. 390, n. 2.

[58] On this see J. C. Plumpe, *Mater Ecclesia: An inquiry into the concept of the Church as mother in early Christianity* (Washington: Catholic University of America Press, 1943), p. 255.

ish) people to which he himself belonged and from which Simon is descended, from whom came the Simonians; and Clobius, from whom the Cleobians came; and Dositheus, from whom the Dositheans came; and Gorthaeus, from whom the Goratheni came; and Masbotheus, from whom the Mosbotheans came. From these [sects] sprang the Menandrianists, Marcionists, Carpocratians, Valentinians, Basilidians, and Saturnilians. Privately and separately each introduced his own peculiar opinion, and from these came the false Christs, false prophets and false apostles, who disrupted the unity of the Church and corrupt speech against God and his Christ.

To be understood correctly this passage must be read in context. The dreadful confusion with which Hegesippus combines the various heresies with which he is acquainted into a genealogical category and links them to Jewish sects[59] and to a legendary arch heretic (whose name and existence is probably due to a misunderstanding)[60] is unsurpassed and is typical of the entire species of polemical literature.[61] It is clear that by doing this the intention is to portray the rise of all heresies as a subsequent degeneration which—in typical fashion[62]—is attributed to the despicable motive of frustrated ambition. No one would want to attempt to authenticate the construed heresiological connections by means of historical research. But yet it should not be overlooked how closely and integrally the details about the orthodox tradition of the Jerusalem church have been woven into worthless reports, and one simply cannot accept these reports uncritically. The first obviously unhistorical assertion made here is that James is considered to be the first bishop of Jerusalem. Schwartz says that this needs

[59] Justin, *Dialog with Trypho*, 80, 4, also mentions seven, but in a more reasonable context.

[60] Cf. Schoeps, *op. cit.*, pp. 283 f. Hilgenfeld and Brand trace the name Thebutis, mentioned only here, to baptism. Only Schoeps associates it with blasphemy.

[61] Cf. especially Eduard Schwartz, *Zwei Predigten Hippolyts* (1936), pp. 30 f.

[62] Cf. Tertullian, *De Baptismo*, 17, 2: "Emulation of the episcopal office is the mother of schisms."

"no further refutation" [63] (even though Caspar is not so sure.) [64] Hegesippus himself, in another context, regards James not as a monarchical, ruling bishop, but as one who receives the church from the Lord "together with the apostles" (i.e., with the Twelve). [65] Nonetheless he very briefly summarizes the details about the succession of James in this passage and emphasizes the unanimity with which Symeon was elevated to the episcopate. Hegesippus uses this election as the cause of the impious rebellion of "Thebutis." In his own account of the incident, Eusebius' construction of the events of this time is even more detailed, and it seems reasonable to assume that his version is nothing more than an elaboration of Hegesippus' account, interlaced with further independent combinations and doubtful conclusions. Hegesippus cannot be regarded as a reliable source for the rest. [66] Eusebius knows of a report stating that a number of the apostles and disciples who were still living and a large number of Jesus' relatives traveled from far and wide and were present at the election. Eusebius states further that they were unanimously agreed upon Symeon, who—and at this point Hegesippus is cited in support—was related to Joseph through his father and was eminently worthy of occupying the throne of the Jerusalem church. [67] It appears that Eusebius himself saw the throne of the episcopacy [68] which James received from Jesus and the apostles. This throne was displayed to visitors whom it impressed as a priceless relic and as a link with the church's past. [69] We do not have to refute the authenticity of this throne, but we should not take too

[63] Eduard Schwartz, *Einleitung zu Eusebius Kirchengeschichte* (1909), pp. ccxxvi f.

[64] I cannot understand how Caspar (*Bischofslisten,* p. 336, n. 4) hopes to impose limitations upon Schwartz's conclusions.

[65] *Historia Ecclesiae,* II, 23, 4.

[66] Except "perhaps Africanus," according to Harnack, *Chronologie,* I, p. 220, n. 1.

[67] *Historia Ecclesiae,* III, 11.

[68] *Ibid.,* VII, 19.

[69] *Ibid.,* VII, 19. But Eusebius is not quite convinced that this is the case. *Historia Ecclesiae,* II, 23, 1. Cf. Caspar, *Bischofsliste,* p. 240, n. 1.

seriously the further details which Eusebius rather uncertainly places at our disposal,[70] nor should we be unduly concerned about the location, the electoral body, or the manner of Symeon's election.[71] Eusebius' account rests on presuppositions which were current in his day that there was a close connection between the original congregation and the worldwide missionary journeys of the apostles. The question which concerns us from a historical point of view is whether the statements of Hegesippus are trustworthy.

James was certainly never the "bishop," patriarch, or high priest of Jerusalem. The assertion that Symeon was his successor (an assertion which was made from the standpoint of the later second century) could be taken seriously only if it could be supposed that episcopal or some other form of ecclesiastical monarchy had taken root in Jerusalem earlier than elsewhere in the church. There is simply no reason for this supposition. Moreover, it is precisely the list of bishops of Jerusalem which presents the most serious obstacles to adopting this view.[72] This list cites thirty names: fifteen Jewish bishops before, and fifteen Gentile bishops after the destruction of Jerusalem. This list ends with Narcissus, the first bishop about whom there are reliable records at the beginning of the third century. When one takes into account that James was murdered during the decade of the sixties of the first century, and that Symeon, his successor, is said to have been martyred under Trajan, this means (and this occurred to Eusebius) that these bishops must have been *komide brachubioi* [very short

[70] According to Harnack (*Chronologie*, I, 128 n. 1), Eusebius introduces a passage with the formula *logos katechei* primarily when he is uncertain of the source on which his assertion rests. For H. J. Lawlor (*Eusebiana*, 1912), this introduction means *Hegesippos istsrei*. In any case, the term is ambiguous. Cf. P. N. Harrison, *Polycarp's Two Epistles to the Philippians* (1936), pp. 214-17.

[71] As is Lohmeyer, *op. cit.*, p. 57, and Schoeps, *op. cit.*, p. 283.

[72] Concerning this list see Harnack, *Chronologie*, I, 97-99, 218-30; C. H. Turner, "The Early Episcopal Lists II: The Jerusalem List," in *The Journal of Theological Studies* (1900), pp. 529-53; Eduard Schwartz, *Einleitung*, pp. ccxxvi f.; and especially Caspar, *Bischofsliste*, pp. 122-32.

lived]. Each of them held office for an average period of no more than three or four years. The list is obviously too long and includes names which later were inserted into the ranks of monarchical bishops. Zahn's assumption[73] that the list erroneously included the names of monarchical bishops of other congregations is an unlikely rationalization. Harnack's assumption,[74] taken over from Knopf,[75] that the explanation for the number of bishops lies in the inclusion of all the *desposunoi* breaks down because this hypothesis can be applied only to the first (i.e., Jewish-Christian) part of the list; and because the excess of names is just as great in the list of later Gentile bishops of Aelia mentioned in the second part. There is just one possible way to preserve the idea of a monarchical order—not entirely, but at least in the early stages—in the structure of the Jerusalem congregation. That would be to assume that there may have been a unique, *ad interim* principle of organization which later was ineffective, i.e., a caliphate. No one, however, has advanced this possibility and this speaks against its probability.

At this point it is necessary to emphasize most strongly that the questionable passage in Hegesippus, which we discussed earlier, is the only account which can be cited in support of a hereditary episcopal succession in the Jerusalem congregation. Schlatter's combinations,[76] that even Symeon's successor, "Juda Justus," could have been a relative of Jesus, is completely untenable. Zahn[77] refuted this idea quite convincingly.[78] Moreover, as we have seen, even the other accounts concerning the *desposunoi* are not strong enough to support the idea of a caliphate. Hegesippus reveals his intense interest in the bio-

[73] Zahn, *op. cit.*, pp. 297 ff.

[74] *Chronologie*, I, p. 220, n. 2; more cautiously in *Die Mission*, p. 631.

[75] *Op. cit.*, pp. 27 f.

[76] *Op. cit.*, pp. 29 ff.

[77] I should not have allowed this possibility to stand in my revision of Karl Müller's *Kirchengeschichte*, I, 1 (3rd ed., 1941), p. 76.

[78] *Op. cit.*, pp. 291 ff. Schoeps agrees that this "is pure phantasy and has no substantiation whatsoever in fact." *Op. cit.*, p. 246.

graphical legend and the family ties which were supposed to have existed in the Jerusalem congregation when in emphasizing the appropriateness of Symeon's election, he states that Symeon, like James, was a relative of the Lord. (This interest dominated the later development of the legend with an increasing lack of restraint.) So, then, it is not possible to salvage from Hegesippus' account any reliable facts in support of a hereditary episcopate. By that I do not wish to deny that Symeon's name may indeed have been passed on to him by reliable sources, or that Symeon could have been a cousin of James. As doubtful as the details are,[79] even Symeon's martyrdom may have some basis in fact. But that is far from meaning, as Hegesippus holds, that Symeon was actually a monarchical bishop of Jerusalem, and that as such he was not only James's successor in the episcopal office, but was his hereditary successor as well. Such an assumption would arbitrarily overthrow the history of the organizational structure of the Jerusalem church which has been established with some degree of certainty by historical research.

The question still remains whether Symeon, possibly even before Hegesippus, was regarded as a guardian of the doctrinal tradition stemming from James. The Jewish-Palestinian setting makes this concept of tradition and succession seem plausible.[80] Caspar's conjecture (highly improbable in itself) that the more or less reliable lists of non-office-holding bearers of tradition preceded the oldest list of bishops could conceivably be correct in this one instance. But we are only groping in the dark with such conjectures. When the old Jewish-Christian tradition in the Pseudo-Clementine epistles speaks about a transmission of apostolic doctrine through James, it is not thinking

[79] Cf. n. 20.

[80] Cf. Wilhelm Bacher, *Tradition und Tradenten in den Schulen Palästinas und Babyloniens* (Berlin, 1914); J. Ranft, *Der Ursprung des katholischen Traditionsprinzips* (1931), pp. 152 ff.; E. Kohlmeyer, *op. cit.*, pp. 235 ff.; and Ethelbert Stauffer, *Die Theologie des Neuen Testaments* (5th ed.; Gütersloh, 1948), pp. 214 f.

about a successor in a "monarchical" sense,[81] and least of all in a hereditary sense.[82] It is rather the seventy disciples,[83] looked upon as prototoypes of the later Jewish-Christian rabbinate,[84] who are the heirs of this tradition and qualified to teach it.[85] This means that the Palestinian development corresponds thoroughly with that in other places, and particularly with that of Rome. I Clement (22:4; 44) corroborates this thesis by indicating that the idea of passing on the tradition is older even in Rome than the idea of a monarchical-episcopal succession. Furthermore, it is made clear that this tradition is not confined to particular individuals, but to the whole body of office-bearers, the *tagma* of the non-monarchical *episkopoi* and *diakonoi*. We see then, that it is hardly possible to regard Symeon as a successor to James even in the sense of being a successor in the matter of doctrine. All we can safely assume is that Symeon enjoyed some kind of prominence in the primitive church in the period immediately after James. His martyrdom would indicate the possibility that he even played a major role. He may have been a "teacher," an "elder," or, as occasion demanded, an apostle[86] in a broader sense of the word. But more than this cannot be said. Only this much is clear: he

[81] *Recognitions* 4, 35 does make mention of a successor—quite naturally an episcopal one—to James. But only Schoeps regards this as belonging to the early stratum of tradition. He regards it as a reference to the later bishop at Pella (*op. cit.*, p. 292). Furthermore, *Contestatio*, 2 f., also assumes that the bishops exercised control over the teachers.

[82] The assumption that at least the right to teach was passed on from father to son, and that this was the usual procedure, seems quite natural in Judaism; but this was not regarded as a foregone conclusion just because it was natural. For further light on this problem see Gerhard Kittel, "Die *genealogiai* der Pastoralbriefe" in *Zeitschrift für die neutestamentliche Wissenschaft*, 20 (1921), 54 ff.

[83] *Contestatio*, 2.

[84] Schmidt, *op. cit.*, p. 316, and Schoeps, *op. cit.*, p. 290. On the basis of this evidence it would be a mistake to attempt to ascertain every detail, e.g., the number of persons constituting an allegedly authoritative Jewish-Christian *Collegium*.

[85] *Homily* 18, 7; cf. *epistula Petri*, 1 f.

[86] For the use of this term in the second century cf. Hans von Campenhausen, "*Der urchristliche Apostelbegriff*," in *op. cit.*, p. 109.

cannot have been the successor to James in either any official or hereditary sense, and for us this is the decisive factor.

The concept of a caliphate or of a hereditary succession of rulers never existed in primitive Christianity. In view of the many colorful lines of development open to early Christianity, some will be reluctant to abandon the remote possibility of a caliphate. Had scholars not been fascinated by the baroque fantasy and appeal inherent in the idea of a caliphate, an idea which fits so well into the Jewish-Oriental milieu of early Christianity, they would not have overlooked the inadequacies of its sources and toyed with the idea for so long. Possibilities, however interesting they may be, cannot be determinative for the historian. Facts are determinative; they are interesting enough.

THE CIRCLE AND THE ELLIPSE

Rival Concepts of Authority
in the Early Church

by Henry Chadwick

THE origins of the papacy have long remained an area of controversial debate for theologians and historians. Yet it ought to be possible for historical theology to cut across the confessional differences and to examine the question on the one hand *sine ira et studio*, [and] on the other hand without the skeptical detachment which says in effect, A plague on both your houses! How was it that the see of Rome came to occupy so important a position in the ancient Catholic church?

Primitive Christianity is a circle with Jerusalem at its center. The first Christians were Jews divided from their fellow countrymen only by the fact that they believed the long expectations of God's people had indeed been fulfilled: Jesus of Nazareth was God's anointed. A prophet had risen up among them, God had visited his people. But this event did not abrogate the past. It was a fulfillment of God's plan. The earliest Christians were not conscious of any discontinuity between the new and the old covenant. The word was still to Israel, and they understood their task as a mission to their own nation, none of whom were likely to be persuaded by an announcement that the Mosaic law had now been abrogated.

Very early within the primitive church at Jerusalem there appeared disturbing men who despaired of the conversion of their own people and believed that the failure of Jerusalem to recognize the things belonging to its peace was theologically significant. According to St. Stephen the failure of Israel to recognize the Messiah is but one more example of that agelong resistance to the prophetic message that may be discerned throughout the Old Testament: the history of the Jews is a long catalog of apostasy from the golden calf to the building of the Temple and the offering of sacrifices. It is not odd that St. Stephen was stoned to death if St. Luke's account of his speech is correct. In any event, some of those who first launched the mission to the Gentiles felt that they should shake the dust of Jerusalem from their feet and take the light of the gospel to lighten the Gentiles.

The Gentile mission was launched gradually on the initiative of private individuals moving ahead of any official authorization by central authority. It was regarded with anxiety at Jerusalem, where conservative Christians thought the Gentile converts ought to be treated like Jewish proselytes and accept the Mosaic law of circumcision and Sabbath observance. For us only one point in this well-worn story is significant: St. Paul's account of his private meeting with the "pillar" apostles presupposes that it was vital to the success of his labors in the Gentile mission, with which he was now identified, that the Jerusalem church should recognize his converts as true and full members, albeit extra-mural members, of the one church of God. Otherwise he would be running and would have run in vain. To the apostle's gratification and also perhaps his astonishment James, Peter, and John made no demand that Gentile Christians must keep the Mosaic law but gave him the right hand of fellowship, laying down only the one condition, that the Gentile communities should show their solidarity with the Jerusalem church by sending money, just as the synagogues of the Jewish dispersion sent annual contributions for the Temple. The epistles offer abundant testimony to show the importance of the collection for the saints in symbolizing the solidarity between Gentile Christians and the Jerusalem community. Even when relations with a church like that at Corinth had become severely strained, St. Paul felt he had to persist in calling on them for contributions, however tortuous and embarrassing his request (witness the syntax of II Cor. 8—9), and however doubtful that the Jerusalem church would be pleased to accept the money at his hands (Rom. 15:31).

The entire story has a single theological presupposition at its foundation: Christendom has a geographical center and this is Jerusalem. Gentile Christians might be free from Judaism, [but] they remained debtors to Zion.

The predominant position of the Jerusalem community was deeply affected by the two Jewish revolts, with the consequent destruction of much of the city and Hadrian's exclusion of all Jews from the new foundation of Aelia Capitolina. Even so there were parts of the old city that remained unharmed. One of its seven synagogues was quite untouched. The Temple area itself was damaged rather than razed to the ground. Admittedly Eusebius of Caesarea grieves over the sad sight of stones from the Temple used for the construction of Hadrian's pagan temples and theaters. But much still remained; and more could be exploited for credulous tourists. The Bordeaux pilgrim of 333 was shown four notable items: the room in which Solomon had written the Book of Wisdom, gruesome traces of Zachariah's murder before the altar, the pinnacle from which the Lord had been tempted to cast himself down, and the very stone which the builders had rejected. More reliable evidence is supplied by Cyril of Jerusalem and John Chrysostom. Commenting on Christ's prophecy that one stone shall not be left upon another, they explain that this is yet to be fulfilled since substantial parts of the old Temple are still identifiable. In a word, much was left to give a sense of continuity with what had gone before. Likewise the church of Jerusalem continued, though now an exclusively Gentile community. All the evidence goes to show that this Gentile church of Jerusalem rapidly became deeply conscious of itself as the inheritor of the most primitive traditions of Christendom. Here was holy ground where the sacred feet of Christ and his apostles had walked not long before. In the third century they claimed to have salvaged the very throne on which James had sat to preach the word to his people. The claim may have been true, since their little church was located in an undevastated part of the old city—on the site, they believed, of that upper room where the gift of the Spirit had been poured out at Pentecost.

The sense of a numinous aura attaching to the church of Zion was not confined to Christians who lived there. It was shared by many throughout the Near East. The first pilgrim to the holy places of whom we have record is Bishop Melito of Sardis, about 170. Forty years later we hear of Alexander, a Cappadocian bishop who, having received the attractive but uncanonical proposal of a transfer to the see of Jerusalem, was granted a revelation directing him to accept it. In the mid-third century Origen and Firmilian, bishop of Cappadocian Caesarea, had a strong interest in the holy places. We know of these four names by chance: the fact of their pilgrimage is recorded by writers primarily interested in telling us something else about them. It is safe to conclude that the volume of devout tourism must have been much greater than these isolated examples might suggest; no one saw anything noteworthy in the mere fact of pilgrimage as such.

We may take it as certain that the visitors would have been specially interested in the continuity of the church with the original community of apostolic times. Melito went to discover the true limits of the Old Testament canon; Firmilian was interested in the ancient liturgy of the Jerusalem church. The lavish benefactions of Constantine and his mother laid great emphasis on the places of Christ's birth and death, and did much to publicize the sacred sites. Constantine's personal sense of the holiness of Palestine comes out in the explanation he gave for the postponement of his baptism until his death-bed: it had been his desire to be baptized in Jordan. But all this only illustrates the mystique. Constantine does not create the Jerusalem idea; he is dependent upon an existing way of thinking, a way of thinking illustrated by the widely held belief that Golgotha (rather than the Temple, as the Jews thought) was the site of Adam's grave and the very center of the earth.

In a word, the original predominance of Jerusalem in the thought of the church did not die with the surrender to Titus' legions or with the Hadrianic war. The city remained at the very heart of things. All this, of course, is in one sense poetry rather than truth, literature rather than dogma, symbol rather than cold reality. But the myth is what matters, and can dominate the minds of those who do not actually believe it. The most extreme mythological account of the central role of Jerusalem in the divine plan is the idea unhappily known as chiliasm or millenarianism; that is, the belief that the Lord will return to reign with his saints for a thousand years in a renewed Jerusalem, a notion fostered by the Apocalypse, regarded as orthodoxy by Justin Martyr, Irenaeus, Tertullian, and even the young Augustine. Even Cyril of Jerusalem in the middle of the fourth century, who did not regard the Apocalypse as canonical scripture and was no millenarian, thinks of his city as the scene of an imminent eschatological conflict, when there will be fighting between the saints of the Jerusalem church and antichrist with his Jewish supporters. It was widely believed that the Lord's second coming would take place at Jerusalem. Tertullian tells us that during Severus' campaigns the new Jerusalem appeared hovering in the sky over Judaea every morning for forty days, visible even to heathen observers. As day advanced the vision slowly faded, though, he adds, on some days it vanished instantly. The Lord was expected to come from the East with the cross preceding him—a belief, first attested in the *Didache*, which explains why Christian places of worship have normally been built so that the worshipers pray eastward and have a cross at the east end. The cross, so Cyril of Jerusalem told his flock, was the sign of the Son of Man (Matt. 24:30), and they believed him. At 9 A.M. on Tuesday, May 7, 351, a parhelion appeared in Palestine and seemed like a cross of light in the east. The terrified citizens of Jerusalem stampeded into church thinking it the sign of the End. In the sobriety of the morning after Cyril assured them that the Lord's return was deferred, but the sign was an assurance that he was indeed on the way.

These examples, selected from much other evidence, illustrate the continuity of the Jerusalem idea. "We make offering for Zion," says the liturgy of St. James, "the mother of all churches." The fact that the administration and effective power in the East was organized around the great sees of Alexandria, Antioch, and Constantinople did not diminish the magnetism of this mystique.

And yet there was one qualification to this claim to be the mother of all churches. The church of Aelia was an exclusively Gentile community, and Aelia was not the secular capital of the Gentile world. That lay in the West; and Rome too was the center of a mystique, potentially a rival mystique.

The story of the Rome idea runs parallel to that of the Jerusalem idea, except that perhaps its controversial potentialities began to be exploited earlier. From the First Epistle of Clement to the Corinthians, it appears that already at the end of the first century the Christians in Rome were taking their leading position for granted, and were looking back with proud local patriotism on the fact that the two most eminent apostles, St. Peter and St. Paul, had been martyred within their city. A century or so later, memorial monuments were erected to the apostles' honor, St. Peter's on the Vatican hill and St. Paul's by the road to Ostia. These monuments are mentioned about A.D. 200 by the Roman presbyter Gaius, and the recent excavations under St. Peter's have unearthed the actual remains of the Petrine monument. The construction of these memorials reflects a growing self-consciousness that the Roman church has a distinguished past.

For the Western churches it always seemed natural to look to Rome as the *prima cathedra*. The church there was the headquarters from which the Christian mission spread through the Western provinces, and no other [Western] city could make any plausible claim to apostolic origin. The Roman church was the only Western community to whom St. Paul had addressed an epistle, and it was proud of the fact. Christians elsewhere instinctively share this sense of respect for the church which preserved the memory of the teaching and practice of St. Peter and St. Paul. Bishop Polycarp of Smyrna traveled to Rome to discuss differences in observing Easter; he and Bishop Anicetus agreed to differ, since both had to follow the traditions of their own apostles. A generation later such divergence seemed intolerable; Bishop Victor of Rome excommunicated all who did not follow the Roman Easter. We are not told the reasons he gave, if any, for taking this short way with dissenters; but the fact that the bishop of Ephesus answered his "threats" by appealing to the tombs of Philip and John in Asia suggests that Victor had appealed to St. Peter and St. Paul; he must have believed he was observing Easter in the way the apostles had done. A few years later we have the fragments of the Dialogue between the Roman presbyter Gaius and a Montanist from Asia Minor named Proclus, where the disputants made rival claims to apostolic foundations. Proclus vindicated the apostolic tradition of the Asian churches and the proper place of prophecy within church life by appealing to the tombs of Philip and his daughters in Phrygia. The Roman, however, could point proudly to the memorials of the martyred apostles, St. Peter and St. Paul—those, he said, with pardonable exaggeration, who "founded this church"—and add, for good measure, that the superiority of the Roman church to the Eastern churches is also proved by the mistake of the benighted Orientals who imagined St. Paul to be the author of the Epistle to the Hebrews. Rome knew better than that.

Victor's actions disclosed to the Greek East that Rome was thinking of Christendom as a circle now centered upon itself. The Eastern churches thought rather of an ellipse with two foci. The legacy of this controversy is disastrously apparent in the centuries that followed. In the middle years of the third century there was sharp controversy concerning the rebaptism of those baptized by schismatics, and against the claims of Rome to settle the controversy over the heads of the dissenting Africans, Cyprian appealed for support to Eastern bishops. We possess the letter written to him by Firmilian of Cappadocian Caesarea, mentioned earlier as a pilgrim to the holy land. He tells Cyprian that the Roman bishop's claim to observe the liturgical customs of the apostles is proved false by this significant fact: "They do not do everything exactly as it is done at Jerusalem." The latent resentment flared into open war in the Arian controversy. In 340 Pope Julius admitted to communion some bishops who for various reasons, not all discreditable, had been excommunicated by Eastern councils, and justified his action by the dignity attaching to the church of St. Peter and St. Paul. The Eastern bishops were horrified. For Rome, they said, we have profound regard as a center of orthodoxy from apostolic times; but the bishop of Rome will remember that the apostles went to Rome from the East. The Eastern bishops took it for granted that the bishop of Rome was patriarch of the West and bishop of the world's greatest city, of a church that could justly take pride in its apostolic origin and noble fight for the faith. The bishop of Rome took it for granted that he was at the center of the circle, successor of the prince of the apostles. And if it was asked wherein lies the superiority of Rome to Antioch, of which Peter had also been bishop, the answer came that Rome's unique distinction lies in the possession of the remains of the martyred apostles. Rome had got the bones.

The tension concerning Easter was decided in favor of Rome. In the fourth century further disagreement arose over the observance of the Nativity. Western custom was now to keep December 25 as Christ's birthday; but about the same time the Eastern churches had come to observe this feast on January 6. Gradually the feast of the Epiphany made its way into Western churches, either as a commemoration of Christ's baptism or as a celebration of the visit of the Magi. But there was some resistance to the Epiphany festival in the West, notably among sects that had separated from the church before

the feast came in. St. Augustine attacked the African Dona-
tists on the interesting ground that their refusal to keep
Epiphany proved their schismatic character; they could not
be members of the universal church if they were out of step
with the church of Jerusalem where the star of the Nativity
appeared. (The point, incidentally, illustrates the perennial
truth that sects remain conservative, while the church moves
with the times.) Likewise in the East, the Western festival
of December 25 made its way slowly. The strongest resistance
came from Jerusalem, which only introduced the festival in
the middle of the fifth century, probably after the council of
Chalcedon, and from Armenia, which to this day does not
keep the Nativity on the Western date.

Western writers long remained sensitive on the score of the
original primacy of Jerusalem. It is noticeable with what pleas-
ure Jerome and Leo drew attention to any defections from
the strict path of orthodoxy on the part of Eastern bishops in
general and bishops of Jerusalem in particular. The Eastern
bishops on their side resented what they regarded as high-
handed interference from the Western patriarch. At the second ecumenical Council at Constantinople in 381 a proposal
to reach a settlement acceptable to the West was met with the
cry: "Christ came in the East!" It was one thing for this
argument to be used by Eastern bishops. It was another when
the same argument was used by bishops in Gaul or England
in order to deflate the claims of Rome in Europe. Saint
Columban wrote angrily to the pope early in the seventh
century, reminding him that though Rome was a famous
church, justly proud of its secular dignity and its relics of
St. Peter and St. Paul, nevertheless it yielded the primacy to
Jerusalem. The same argument recurs in the York Tracts of
about 1100, perhaps the work of the then archbishop of
Rouen. When we hear this sort of thing from the West, we
may fairly conclude that something like Gallicanism or even
Anglicanism had already been born.

It would be tempting to continue by observing how in the
modern world the ideological tension between East and West

has become secularized in the form of competition between Russia and America. But I beg leave to resist these temptations, and rather to invite you to go back in time and to examine the roots of this cleavage, the development of which I have attempted to trace. I submit that the seeds of the subsequent development are in the New Testament.

St. Paul, as we have seen, had to gain the recognition of the Jerusalem authorities if his Gentile converts were to be admitted as full members of the church. He was continually stressing the need for unity in the church, and the solidarity of the Gentile Christians which the church of Jerusalem expressed through the collection for the saints. St. Paul himself had a deep instinctive respect for Jerusalem and for the church leaders there which may be discerned behind his ironical references to "those who seemed to be pillars." Nevertheless, he also affirmed (in Galatians stridently asserts), his own independent and equal standing as an apostle on a par with the others. According to Galatians 2[:9], James, Cephas, and John gave Paul the right hand of fellowship, recognizing that he had been entrusted with the apostleship of the Gentiles just as St. Peter had been entrusted with that of the Jews. In the mind of St. Paul this was certainly more than an allocation of different spheres of activity; it implied a paralled status between Jewish and Gentile Christendom. The circle was already on the way to becoming an ellipse.

A second piece of evidence is provided by Romans 9–11. There St. Paul wrestles with the problem of the failure of God's elect people to believe in the Christ of expectation. Why had the Jews failed to believe? The answer is that they had been temporarily blinded, and the light had passed to the Gentiles to provoke the Jews to jealousy, to wake them up to their responsibilities that they should be a light to lighten the Gentiles. At the same time the Gentile Christians must remember the rock whence they have been hewn, must not become conceited or proud of their privilege in receiving the gospel when the elect nation has rejected it, and must realize that God's promise to his chosen will finally be fulfilled. In the end all Israel will be saved, together with "the fullness of the Gentiles." The position of Gentiles within the people of God is compared to that of a branch grafted into a vine, which may be cut off if it proves unfruitful. Gentile Christianity is a parenthetic, Protestant movement to recall Catholic Judaism to its true vocation.

In St. Paul's mind there was a duality in the idea of the church. On the one hand there is his assertion of the need for recognition by the church of Jerusalem; on the other hand he was deeply aware of the equal status of the Gentiles within the one commonwealth of God. The idea of two distinct entities within the one church was widely current in the second and third centuries. For example, the Alexandrian exegetes significantly expounded St. Matthew's account of the triumphal entry into Jerusalem to the effect that the colt and the foal symbolize two churches, Jewish and Gentile, who in double harness draw the chariot of the Lord's triumph. But this kind of exegesis was not to last long. Soon the Gentile Christians came to constitute an overwhelming majority. "Christian Jews," Origen sadly observes, "are very rare." They never had any great success in their mission to their fellow countrymen; they were suspect for lack of patriotism, in that the Jerusalem church had left the city when the war began in A.D. 66 and retired to Pella in Transjordan, and were again killed off as fifth-columnists during the second revolt of Bar-Cochba, as we know from Justin Martyr and (if correctly interpreted) from the autograph letter of Bar-Cochba himself recently discovered in the Judaean desert. They were even more suspect for their attitude to the Gentile mission, to the approval of which they were committed by the Apostolic Council. We know that in the fourth century the Jewish Christian communities were proud of the missionary achievements of St. Paul, even if they must at times have regarded him as a gift horse whose mouth needed close inspection. Unfortunately, the Gentile Christians were less tolerant. Justin Martyr had to admit that, while he himself did not object to Jewish Christians who continued in the observance of the

Mosaic law, some Gentile Christians denied them all hope of salvation. It was the latter view, not Justin's, which became predominant. It is the complete reversal of the situation that had confronted St. Paul when he went up to confer with James, Cephas, and John a century earlier. It was now for the Jewish Christians to seek recognition from the Gentiles, and they sought it largely in vain.

It is a short step from this position to the identification of Christianity with Gentile Christendom *tout court*. This identification is made easier by the widely held conviction that in the providence of God the destinies of the church and the empire were bound up together. At least by the middle of the second century and perhaps much earlier Christians were already looking forward to the day when the Roman emperor himself would be converted to the faith. Is it not providential, asked Melito of Sardis, that Augustus established the Pax Romana at the same time as the birth of Christ's religion of peace? Nearer and nearer was drawing the time when the earth would be full of the knowledge of the Lord as the waters cover the sea. With the conversion of Constantine the dream came true. To Ambrose, *Romanus* and *Christianus* are interchangeable terms. To Leo, St. Peter and St. Paul were the new Romulus and Remus, founders of Christian Rome. The African Optatus instinctively treated the barbarians outside the empire as being beyond the scope of the gospel. Christianity belonged to the Roman world. We are assisting at the birth of "Western values."

The apostle Paul was the creator of the idea of a quasi-independent Gentile Christendom within the one church of Jewish and Gentile believers, and for him this stood or fell with recognition of his own apostolate. What, then, was his own attitude to the capital city of the Gentile world? Among the motives that led him to write the epistle to the Romans a large place must be given to the assertion of his authority in relation to the Roman church. In Romans 15:14 ff. he tells the Roman Christians that, although they are indeed so mature as scarcely to require his instruction, "yet on certain points I have written to you very boldly, by way of reminder, because of the grace given to me by God to be a minister of Christ Jesus to the Gentiles. . . ." Now he has finished his labors in the East and "having longed for many years to come to you" will make the journey as soon as he has delivered the collection for the saints at Jerusalem, if the church there will accept it, and if he is not lynched by the unbelieving Jews on arrival. (Evidently St. Paul knew that the welcome barometer is near zero.) In case the Romans felt a little apprehensive they were assured that he would soon be off again on a missionary tour of Spain—an assurance in which, as John Chrysostom pointed out, there was probably more than meets the eye. We may be sure that the central goal in the apostle's mind was Rome rather than the Costa Brava.

The epistles tell us nothing of the way in which Paul reached Rome. But in the last eight chapters of the Acts we have a very remarkable account of his journey. As he had himself feared, he was attacked by the unbelievers and only rescued by the Roman military authorities putting him under arrest. From then on, St. Luke's story is the account of a journey overruled and guided through a series of dramatic crises by the intervention of providence. Humanly speaking the apostle stood not the remotest chance of reaching Rome at all. A succession of divinely inspired situations enabled him to circumvent all the obstacles, ultimately to arrive at the capital, there to preach boldly, no man forbidding him. The key to the story is the account of the storm and shipwreck in Acts 27. It is unfortunate that this chapter has been misunderstood by commentators. The story occupies a quite disproportionate amount of space, and one asks why St. Luke thought it so important. The commentaries either tell us that the story is there because it is an eyewitness acount—it happened—or that it was invented by a fertile imagination, constructed out of the literary conventions of contemporary adventure stories. The answer is surely that the story is there to underline the extreme improbability that the apostle would ever reach Rome. The very stars in their courses were fighting against him. When land had nearly been reached, only the centurion's intervention prevented the soldiers from killing the prisoners. When they landed on Malta, there was a serpent to bite him. For the author of Acts the preaching of the apostle of the Gentiles in the capital of the Gentile world was a supernatural fact.

Dean Inge once remarked that the apostle Paul has never been a very popular saint in the Roman Catholic Church. "St. Peter," he continued characteristically, "the Blessed Virgin, and a host of lesser lights have been wheedled and cajoled. St. Paul has been spared this crowning humiliation." The point could be more irenically put. Let it simply be said that the visitor to Rome who passes from the great church of St. Peter's to that of St. Paul's-without-the-Walls is struck by the isolation and neglect of the latter. There is perhaps irony here. For if there is one man who more than any other one man may be regarded by the historian as founder of the papacy, that man is surely St. Paul.

For Further Reading

CULLMAN, OSCAR. *Peter, Disciple, Apostle, Martyr.* Translated by
F. V. Filson. London: SCM Press, 1953.

HARNACK, ADOLF VON. *The Constitution and Law of the Church in
the First Two Centuries.* Translated by F. L. Pogson. New
York: G. P. Putman, 1910.

JALLAND, T. G. *The Church and the Papacy.* New York: More-
house-Gorham, 1944.

LIETZMANN, HANS. *A History of the Early Church.* Four volumes
in two. Vol. 1, translated by Bertram Lee Wolf. New York:
The World Publishing Co., 1953.

STREETER, B. H. *The Primitive Church.* New York: Macmillan,
1929.

Facet Books Already Published

13. *The Problem of the Historical Jesus*
    by Joachim Jeremias (translated by Norman Perrin). 1964
14. *A Primer of Old Testament Text Criticism*
    by D. R. Ap-Thomas. 1966
15. *The Bible and the Role of Women*
    by Krister Stendahl (translated by Emilie Sander). 1966

Social Ethics Series:

1. *Our Calling*
   by Einar Billing (translated by Conrad Bergendoff). 1965
2. *The World Situation*
   by Paul Tillich. 1965
3. *Politics as a Vocation*
   by Max Weber (translated by H. H. Gerth and C. Wright Mills). 1965
4. *Christianity in a Divided Europe*
   by Hanns Lilje. 1965
5. *The Bible and Social Ethics*
   by Hendrik Kraemer. 1965
6. *Christ and the New Humanity*
   by C. H. Dodd. 1965
7. *What Christians Stand For in the Secular World*
   by William Temple. 1965
8. *Legal Responsibility and Moral Responsibility*
   by Walter Moberly. 1965
9. *The Divine Command: A New Perspective on Law and Gospel*
   by Paul Althaus (translated by Franklin Sherman). 1966
10. *The Road to Peace*
    by John C. Bennett, Kenneth Johnstone, C. F. von Weizsäcker, Michael Wright. 1966
11. *The Idea of a Natural Order: With an Essay on Modern Asceticism*
    by V. A. Demant. 1966
12. *Kerygma, Eschatology, and Social Ethics*
    by Amos N. Wilder. 1966
13. *Affluence and the Christian*
    by Hendrik van Oyen. 1966
14. *Luther's Doctrine of the Two Kingdoms*
    by Heinrich Bornkamm (translated by Karl H. Hertz). 1966

Type used in this book
Body, 10 on 12 Janson
Display, Janson & Garamond
Paper: White Spring Grove, E. F.